The Missing

SiÂN HuGHES is a lone parent who lives in the middle of nowhere with her two young children and works part time as a teacher and in a book shop/cafe. In 2006 she won the Arvon International Poetry Competition with 'The Send Off', an elegy for her third child.

The Missing

SIÂN HUGHES

CAMBRIDGE

PUBLISHED BY SALT PUBLISHING
14a High Street, Fulbourn, Cambridge CB21 5DH United Kingdom

© Siân Hughes, 2009

The right of Siân Hughes to be identified as the
author of this work has been asserted by her in accordance
with Section 77 of the Copyright, Designs and Patents Act 1988.

Salt Publishing 2009

Printed in Great Britain by the MPG Books Group, Bodmin and King's Lynn

Typeset in Swift 9.5 / 13

ISBN 978 1 84471 498 8 hardback

Salt Publishing Ltd gratefully acknowledges
the financial assistance of Arts Council England

Contents

Acknowledgements

'Secret Lives' won the 1996 TLS / Poems on the Underground competition. 'Cartoon', 'Bear Awareness and Self-Defence Classes' and 'Noises Off' first appeared in *London Magazine*, then in *Saltpetre* (Smith/Doorstop, Huddersfield) along with 'Sleepwalker' and 'Cursing the Holy Ghost'. 'Catalogue', 'The Sacking Offence' and 'Country Compilation' appeared in the *TLS*. 'Easy' was commissioned by the *TES*. 'Propaganda' and 'Electricity' appeared in *The Gift: New Writing for the NHS*, and 'Results' was commissioned by Poems in the Waiting Room. 'The Double at Highbury', 'The Girl Upstairs' and 'Fidelity' appeared in *Anvil New Poets III*. 'Sleep Training' was published by *MsLexia*. 'Aitken Drum' appeared in *The Spectator*. 'The Send-Off' won the Arvon Poetry Competition in 2006 and was published in the competition anthology.

I am grateful for the support of a Southern Arts Writers Award and bursaries from The Arvon Foundation.

The Double at Highbury

The day Arsenal won the double you stayed out of town
while I went looking for a houseboat for one.
It was moored under the tropical aviary at the Zoo
and, having no engine of any kind, was staying there.

The toilet arrangement was a bucket and hose
and relied on the cover of darkness. This was June,
but the owner made light of the way the tin roof
turned it into a floating methane-fuelled oven.

There was a washing-machine, with a patched outlet pipe
and a generator wired to an illegal stand on the tow path.
The owner waved his cigarette in the vague direction
of the single bunk bed and told me to look round.

On the way home I struck lucky in the local hospice shop
with exactly the right kind of shirt for £4. It's amazing
what people throw out. I was home before the whistle,
when shouting and horn-blowing filled the street,

went on until the sirens joined in at eleven. All night
heat held the sounds in close-up. The air would not move.
I waited for you to call so I could hold the receiver
up to the open window and let you into my world.

Catalogue

Your desk faces north, mine faces the wall:
over each of them you hang a picture
of your wife, in case we forget who we are
or what we are doing here. 'After I'm dead,'
you say, 'she'll come back for the library.'

The staircase separates fiction from drafts,
pornography fills the loft. The landing
with a leaking roof (biography, misc.)
is ordered on a private system (by friends,
of friends, for sale, the rest.)

If I take the basement, (romance, plays) you're left
with everything you like to think might be true:
poetry, newspapers, letters, Fine Art, those volumes
in dark covers under the sink, her memoirs, bath books,
city guides, dictionaries, and all the stuff in the attic.

Secret Lives

Sometimes your dressing gown unhooks
and slides out under the garden door
with three aces up his sleeve.

He flies in the face of next door's dog,
back flips down the middle of the street,
opening himself to the breeze.

Something in pink nylon flutters a cuff
from an upstairs window. He twirls his cord
to beckon her outside.

They're heading for a club they know
where the dress code is relaxed midweek,
and the music is strictly soul.

The Girl Upstairs

The girl upstairs wears white lycra shorts
even in winter. 'They're comfy'
she says, 'What's the problem?'
From the back door you can hear
the steady scratch of her electric meter.

The corner shop sends messenger boys
up the road with her grocery boxes.
Cling peaches in syrup, carnation milk,
baby carrots, peas. Her freckles
are pale orange under a homemade tan.

The landlord says 'She could make it nice.
Homely. But she's not the type.'
Her boyfriend laughs. 'When I come home
I don't want gardening and all that crap.
Fornication. That's what a man needs.'

Taxi

In the taxi you say 'I know this part of town,
or I used to, years ago, when I had a tart.
That is the right word for it, isn't it? Tart?'
'Not really,' I say, and unbutton my coat.

'She had a terrible yappy dog, but I didn't care.
She was nice and fat. I liked that. Fat.'
I lift my dress over the tops of my stockings.
'Fat,' you say again. 'Lovely and fat.'

The Greedy Man

The Greedy Man counts boiled eggs
back into their box, eleven,
ten; his tongue plays out

over cooking instructions.
Steam rises. He sighs
as the microwave tray revolves.

He freckles the skin
on a bowl of blancmange
with hundreds and thousands.

'Hundreds and thousands'
he murmurs, delighted
one dish can contain so many.

Easy

The same air we collected
in our hair and clothes
from a view of the river

is flowing out of hedgerows
up the garden wall
through the open window

to and from between our mouths;
thoughtless, nocturnal,
with no sense of occasion,

nothing we said or didn't say
stops it short. It seems content
lifting our ribs, and then letting go.

Noises Off

There's something in my eye,
a smudge over everything
to the left of the television.
I can ignore it if I choose.
A door opens and closes
your side of a long-distance call.

Turn my face to the light.
Tell me there's nothing there.

The Sacking Offence

Like the outline of a paperclip
left on the windowsill two summers ago
or fingerprints, dusted over, but still intact
along the edge of the franking desk,
something like cigarette smoke
might, even this far into the week,
uncurl from the corner of a table,
to print last Friday, ten p.m.
as a row of inverted chimneys
across the calendar on the back wall.

Sleepwalker

At intervals in the night his footsteps
climb the stairs, then change direction.
The cistern empties, pauses and refills.

Before breakfast he turns back the quilt
on her aeroplane pyjamas, biscuit crumbs,
a paperback copy of *The Bald Prima Donna*.

She's taken his favourite pillow next door.
He helps himself to her vanishing cream,
draws the curtains for a morning's sleep.

Saltpetre

You taught me how to roll cigarettes
without saltpetre, the slightest draft blows them out.

I count your visitors in empty bottles, a steady drip
of something collecting under your chair.

There are slates in the guttering, dead leaves
and newspapers behind the door.

I'm preoccupied with the state of your collars,
worn through to the webbing, lost buttons,

the damp under the window, the problem of storage,
the way your shoe heels wear down on a diagonal,

a shadow that falls across your eyes
as if you were watching me undress.

Fidelity

According to the magazine I picked up at the airport
that caramel-brown mongrel who followed you the length of the beach
is the perfect colour for your star sign, one you should wear every day.
He suited you, it's true, his long snout lifted to your waist
as he kept time with your feet, pointer-fashion.
In the evening light the high-stepping ripples of his shadow
as it crossed the tide-marked sand suggested something pedigree.

Today I saw him tack out from behind the windsurf place
and slip into a pack of Germans on their way to the port, his smooth coat
an effortless match for their close-cropped heads and tans.
Long before they loaded the last rucksack onto the pilot boat
he was shedding gold flecks of blond light from his fur,
ducking into the shade behind a stack of blue plastic crates,
his eye on the slow swinging gait of a passing American.

The Stairs

It's one of those parties where the children have taken the seats
in the living room, and no one eats the sandwiches. On the stairs
ex-lovers compete for who looks down on whom. No one consoles
the woman in a low-cut dress sitting outside the bathroom
waiting for her lover to take his wife home.

Her lover's son keeps bringing her cake—she's usually more fun
on their trips to the zoo. The boy wants to play monkeys. Gorillas.
Anything in cages. Her hand is white on the banister.
'Go carefully down the stairs,' she says. 'Hold on tight.'

Shikseh

scrubber, slattern, slag, doxey,
white trash, bit-on-the-side,
—not to be taken home, taken
in your mouth, not to be
taken to heart

a pick-up, practice-run,
on-off-on, part-time,
day-time, texts-only, token gesture:
someone you're sort-of seeing—
but only with one eye.

Propaganda

This is the place where they ask
'Can the doctors write to you
using this name and address?'
before they tick the standard form
and stack it, face down, behind the desk:
where you sit very still on smooth chairs
and reread the horoscopes
in back issues of *Company*:
where someone looks you in the eye
and says 'You do know what I mean
when I say markers in the blood?'
Where you promise to be good
next time, forever, play it safe,
for a string of negatives, a new life.

Results

Of course it was always going to be secret,
an envelope no one would know had arrived
that I'd lock myself in the bathroom to read.

Nothing like coming down late to breakfast
and you saying 'How you failed history
I'll never know.' Or standing in a queue

in the only taverna with a land line,
the owner grinning between black teeth
while I ask you 'How did it go?' and wait

for a pause that might mean well, or not.
Out on the terrace the old dog gets up
and drags his chain two steps into the shade.

You're

my pod, blip, popped balloon
from a cancelled birthday party,

my bubble, bloat, floatation tank,
fault on the radar, jellyfish, dredgeling,

split condom, surgical glove,
sum of subtraction, counting down

from the first of Advent
to flat-as-a-Pancake Day. Zero.

Off the hook, unfished, adrift,
out of trouble, off the diet,

lined up outside the office
for a final dressing down

you're headlong for the nearest exit.

The Night Bus

The last bus out of Dudley Port on Tuesday night
is miles from the shops, flagged down by a woman
so pregnant she has to turn sideways to get on board

and then takes up all three of the seats reserved
for elderly or infirm. She has twelve carrier bags
from Mothercare and Ethel Austin, worn out, faded,

bags full of holes, spilling dusty clothes and nappies.
When she leans back against the window her hair
slips forward over her huge face. She's bright red

except for a three day beard. It doesn't match the wig.
Her support stockings need hitching. A striped pillow
slides out from under the monstrous dressing gown.

And every other sadness that takes the last bus home,
climbs on arguing who has the right change, edges past
her belly, her bags, her smile, stares out of the window

past their own reflection at green power-station clouds
finds their own losses, their missing lives,
too quietly dressed now, shy, undramatised.

Everybody Knows

that Cinderella wears a new dress
and travels in a pumpkin,

that fancy slippers slow you down
when you're chasing midnight,

that the prince has little to say
or do, as long as he likes small feet,

that the girl in the party dress
always meant to leave her number,

that she wants him forever, now
she'll never run away from him again.

Cursing the Holy Ghost

Who would have thought it so easy?
You don't need to go outside,
or raise your voice, he can hear
if you speak it softly, at home in bed,
or if you pretend it isn't that bad
and start by saying 'I love you, but . . .'

You won't know for years if it has worked.
Those voices coming up the stairs at night
might be nothing to do with you.
A sound like glass under somebody's shoe
could be something else entirely.

Country Compilation

There's a 'phone call I'm not making,
a letter that falls off a list of things to do
every day or so. I'd dial the number now
but there's no battery in the remote
and by the end of *Grievous Angel*
you'll be thinking about lunch.

Our lines are surely well rehearsed—
there should be time for congratulations
between *A Lonestar State of Mind*
and that 1956 Elvis
recorded too close to the microphone,
attentive to each breath.

Cartoon

Do you remember that time in *Scooby Doo*
when the gang were trapped in some kind of cave
and Shaggy drew a doorway on the rock face,
turned an imaginary key and walked out?

And do you remember us watching it,
as if it had nothing to do with you,
or me, or the drawings you were doing
even then, first the outline, then the colouring in?

Delivery

I was used to cattle, so I recognised the sound
that came out of me when the cord pulled tight
around his neck and the whole thing stalled.

You can hear them three fields away and more,
a deep bellow like that means they're calving
or else they've gone too far into the marsh,

panicked, eyes rolled wide to the whites, the vet
running in — rope in one hand, shotgun in the other —
as their hooves sink deeper in the mire.

Flood

You were born the time of the floods. We stay home
for ten days and watch the levels rise. Then you get ill.

On the fourth floor of the hospital they put you on a drip
and me on a folding bed, till six, when I pack it away.

The consultant is pregnant, and needs space by your cot,
to read the clip chart, and say 'So far so good'. I can sleep

upright on my plastic chair. I can sleep against a wall.
I sleep through you waking. The night nurse walks you

up and down the ward at three o'clock in one of the prams.
She sings to you. She says you like it. A ride in a pram,

up muddy lanes where the cows breathe over gates,
along the river past houseboats, swans and ducks

and back again across deep blue fields and pathways
skating high above the grass, gravestones, hedges,

through salt-water running over bridges, around trees
foreshortened by flooding, their waterlogged roots

reaching further and further for safety, for dry land.

Electricity

The night staff are peeling off their gowns
and hanging them on the ends of cots;
sleeves of blue and green spotted cows
hang in folds of smiling daisies.

The parents fold camp beds in half
and wheel them into place behind balloons,
streamers, get well cards, soft toys
carrying safety labels and price tags.

They nod to each other, duck their heads
into sheets and blankets, pull them apart
in a shower of sparks. No one speaks
of electricity, their hair standing on end.

Aitken Drum

The older children carry their own drips and lines
down the corridor for activities. Music today,
two people with guitars and a box of percussion
bash out Aitken Drum, once through for each child.

Between choruses they ask for names,
try to pick up the whispers.

You can't join in. You're too young to lift your head,
even if the sound of the gently shaken tambourine
didn't upset you, the way all noise upsets you, even if
you stopped crying, the light stopped hurting your eyes,

if you woke, and told me, in a whisper,
your secret name.

Mengy Babies

Every other day there's a new one, and you're not the worst,
I know, because the nurses took the mobiles from your bed,
and gave them all to Archie. He's nine months old, a giant
next to you, like Finn McCool crammed in his cot, huge head
lolling helpless, full of tubes. His Father comes from work
in a blue overall, and weeps for hours into the monitor.
His mother says 'I kept telling them something's wrong.
I kept phoning and telling them, something's gone wrong.'

Fireworks on Ward 4C

The lights are out in the playroom
where gathered at the windows
on flimsy metal legs, a small crowd
of saline drips and monitors
send out quiet illuminations
in response to the distant trees.

Only the rockets reach us here.
A series of explosions at ground level
do no more than colour the sky dark green
as we wait for the next high-pitched yell
to descend into a whining thump
and a spray of pink and yellow stars.

Dyslexic

You start off learning everything backwards,
crawling upright on your bottom, reversing
into tight corners and down stairs. Up slides,
slowly, and forwards down the ladder.

Words turn around on you, whole sentences
inside out. Until the day you find the ideal path
round the farm away from the older children
through an open gate onto a wet plank bridge

across the lichen-covered silt-black pond.
You step into it neatly up to your neck
and climb out again up a vertical bank
on your belly. Then you call for help.

My Children

were never going to be like that, egg-white
in sunlight, who refuse food, refuse sleep,
projectile vomit, have teeth full of holes,
have special food in sealed containers,
use three dummies at a time, who, when they slip
and fall in the rain, run full pelt down the street
away from me, and won't be comforted.
I was never going to have children who did that.

Bear-Awareness and Self-Defence Classes
or Fathers and Husbands

There is no need to be afraid of the bears.
Most of them will avoid you if they can.
Carry a toy trumpet, tin whistle,
anything you can use as a drum.

First identify your bear. If it's brown,
try shouting, stamping, strike a blow.
Your best bet with a black bear
is lie down quickly and play dead.

Try to resist the urge to run.
Bears are surprisingly quick on their feet,
especially if they're hungry,
angry, frightened or still young.

The Fight

Me every time. Admit it. You laugh
but won't back down.

I compare fists, fitness, weight.
I can't see your advantage.

Masculinity? Practice? Something
you're holding back.

I thought you wanted me stronger,
less sad. I thought this fight

was the one I was meant to go out fighting.

Superking 6 × 6

The new bed is a giant. It's bigger than a king. In fact,
if you were to measure it from side to side and then
in the other direction, you would find it's as broad
as it's long. Six foot one way, half a dozen in the other.
It's as broad as it's long. You stay away. You stay awake.
We take it in turns to be sleepless, unsettled. If push

comes to shove we can always blame the children
for taking up the space in the middle. Six nights of one,
half a dozen of the other. It's at least three beds in one,
yours, mine, and the middle ground. Who's to blame
for the distance to be crossed? It's as broad as it's long,
six feet in one direction, six feet in the other.

Xperiment!

The children turn the duvet inside-out,
ride what's left of its feathers to the floor
to watch breakfast TV—Xperiment!
What's most slippery, custard, banana,
or beans? We don't care. 'Slide!' shouts the baby
as men in wetsuits leap into the food.

The next experiment drops household goods
from a crane. A man in a yellow coat
runs out to measure whose component parts
travel the furthest from a point of impact.
Freezer, piano, double bed: I watch
slow motion replays of crash after crash.

Sleep Training

This is a lifeskill, and I will learn
to go back to sleep without crying.
It is normal to find myself alone
at night. It is normal to call out
and for no one to come. I will adjust.

Already I barely acknowledge the sound
of my screaming, night after night.
It is almost like silence to me, almost
like the night itself. I will learn
to close the door, turn aside, and sleep.

The Send-Off

Mummy has to go now. Sorry we were late.
I brought you a flower. No, it's dead.

When you cut them, you see, they die.
The petals were white when I left.

I was sewing your name tags.
This is your name. I know it's no use to you now.

Home clothes are not allowed. It's the rules.
Your shawl is taped to your parcel.

Don't be afraid. You are not alone,
and no one has a bed with a window.

The man with the spade brings you in
from the rain. The one in black says words.

In a few weeks they'll come back
and let in more new friends.

The view changes each time. The sky,
believe me, is not always this cold.

When I was a little girl like you
I liked to peep through the banisters

and see who was calling so late.
My parents in their fancy clothes

might turn and say 'Who's out of bed?'
The visitors blew kisses. Sometimes

they saved me something special
that the grown-ups had to eat.

My darling, sleep well in your bed.
Don't come out on the landing where it's cold

because, you see, I won't come home
in my long dress and necklace

and blow you kisses up the stairs.
I won't carry you back to bed

to rub your blue feet better
or fetch blankets from the box.

No, you don't need a bottle, cuddle,
special rabbit, teddy, bit of cloth.

You don't even need to close your eyes.
They were born that way, sealed shut.

You are a hard lesson to learn,
soft though you are, and transparent.

There's a mark on your forehead—
the simple flaw that separates
the living from the dead.

It looks like I dropped you downstairs.
I didn't. I promise. It was like this:

somebody did some counting
and when they added you up

they found one part of you didn't match.
It's supposed to come out even.

They call it trisomy twenty-one.
It's not such a lucky number.

No, I know it doesn't begin to explain
your lack of Christmas presents

or the colour of your skin. I know
the best smiles in the world come out uneven.

Sweet Ghost

It turns out you are the quiet one.
The dismantled cot in the landing cupboard
has pieces that rattle. You leave them silent.

The clothes that fly downstairs are thrown
by my hand. I slam doors in my face.
I trip on nothing, choke on clean water.

You might at least throw dirt in my mouth.
Look, it's open. I'm letting in your air.

Storm Clouds

I am not afraid of thunderstorms,
the floods that rise under graves.
I am not afraid of river bank collapses
or burst drains. You do not feel the cold.
You do not see the lightning flash
nor hear the thunder. You'll never count
miles between one and the other.
You are not afraid of the storm.

I am not afraid of storm clouds
or changes in the weather.
The ground opens, and closes over.
No amount of rain will make you grow
or change for the better. There's no need,
my darling, for you or I to be afraid.

Humpty Dumpty (Egg, or Gun)

Something falls, and it stays broken. Gun, or egg,
we send for the cavalry. Uniforms, fanfares, and then
they stand around with their hands in pockets
the horses breathing impatience. No one moves.
No one puts together the pieces that are broken.

Already we are back on that high wall, the view
still long, the shell soft in our hands, the cannon ball
rolling back into the barrel. Egg, or gun,
we all know the story. Something breaks
and nothing will mend it now it is broken.

The Missing

The clocks go back, but not far enough.
We're rattled, unrested, the little one screams.
Our unglued eyes still long for sleep, for more
than only yesterday, for a month of Sundays,

a lifetime. The clocks go back, they scratch
at the surface of yesterday, last night.
It's not enough. All of last month
remains more or less where we left it.

Nativity

We bury you the day before Christmas Eve
but it's not the nativity scenes that get me:
it's a huge plastic Santa strapped to a pub
on the outer ring road, deflating day by day
till he hangs and flaps against the windows
loud and red and wet like a lost glove.

The Return

It's always the same dream. Not the first one, where we are flying
in bigger and bigger circles from the burial ground, backwards,
dizzying, so I'm holding you too tight and you look frightened.

Not that one. The one that comes back is where I find you, safe
in a place for old people and you have never learned to smile.
I have to work out how long you've been there, what you've missed.

And you don't know us, of course, even though we are all there,
and I turn your face to me, tuck the corners of your mouth
into a curve, and start packing your things to come home.

I find a car seat and fasten you into the straps. You're heavy,
but we manage. And then everyone looks at me in an odd way.
Don't I know? It's not possible. No one ever mentioned going home.

Your father says, 'She's fine here, look, she's fine' and sometimes
I cry and disagree, and the old people look embarrassed,
but the ending is always the same. It always ends the same.

Magnetic Fish

The children are playing magnetic fish. Physics
but no biology. Boot. Shark. All in one pot.
They cannot read the numbers. Every catch

is a good catch. It's all a question of holding on.
Boot. Shark. Treasure chest. It's child's play.
A little jump. Then a little holding on.

Not so much hand-to-eye as possession.
Shark. Booty. Jelly fish. Treasure chest.
Every catch is a good catch. A jump. Then holding on.

I Turn Forty

with a cake my mother disowns
seeing how badly it turned out,
who knows, something chemical,
the wind changed, no matter. It's sunk.

She hands out decorations. Fat princess
in a pink dress, a dinosaur no taller,
its toothy mouth wide open, one each
for the children, and one over,

some kind of green monster-bird,
part crocodile, part parakeet.

What If

What if I changed my name, put on weight,
dyed my skin, shaved my head, stopped drinking,
got a new job, a nose job, got into debt, painted
everything bright yellow, moved to another country,
cut out my tongue, grew a new one, grew thinner,
younger, happier, wiped your memory and my own,
drove myself off a cliff, rewound past the beginning
stopped, and started again? What if you were drunk
in a distant seaside bar, and I came in, disguised,
and never turned to face you? Would you, then?
What if I promised nothing would be the same?
What if you made the promises? What then?
What if I never moved from this corner of the room,
never called you, heard you, saw your face again?

Your Advice

The children are potty-trained. They wet the bed
then join me in mine. I'm strict about bed time
so they never come down. I recycle. Glass jars,
bottles, boxes, bath water. I've bought a table saw
and keep the fire lit. At night, while they pee in the dark
alone upstairs, quietly, because I'm being strict,
I bathe in the cold dirty water, sit by the fire
and wait. I'm ready. That could be you. Come in.

Delete

My phone is full of messages from you.
No one calls. They can't. I'm out of order.
It shudders, makes a small protesting sound
as if something were trapped inside. It is.
Seventy messages. Fifty in love,
then the rest that deal with return of clothes.
I copy them out, one by one, retype you,
my fingers follow the path yours followed

letter by letter, line by line, I slide
my fingers down your wrist until my palm
lies underneath your palm. Backspace. Delete.
I'm you and you are loving me. Delete.
Delete. The evidence is in my hand.
Delete. Delete. Delete. Delete. Delete.

The Places for Crying

The car of course. Everyone knows the car.
It beats bathrooms, workrooms, anywhere
you live. It's lockable, and you can get away
from most of the people who see you doing it.

Engine sounds are useful. Music is no good.
Anything with words won't help you. Lights,
queues, politeness, strangers, children, dogs
all make it worse. Except in supermarkets.

Supermarkets work. Open all hours,
with announcements in a foreign voice
you remember from a building site
with chained dogs and sharp-leafed plants

that cut your ankles as you ran away.
You wait your turn now. Your feet hurt.
There's nothing in here that you want to eat.
Hold out your hand. Accept your punishment.

Broken Sonnet

It's no use to anyone. I know that.
Hours go by and nothing moves. Bit by bit

pins and needles take a hold of the feet,
head north, as if it mattered. It doesn't.

I have no excuse for it. No one does.
Time wasted, sleep lost, years and years of it

slipping out the back door of a car
to wave at nobody from the kerbside.

The Theories

There are plenty of them. Injured pride. Old age,
delusion, loneliness, loss of an imagined future
I built around false images of ourselves. But it's you

I miss. The shape of your head, your lip, close up
bread-coloured freckles, smell of your soap. Your voice.
Not what you said. Not the words. The sound of it.

Falling for Elvis

too late of course. I'm old, he's dead,
so I start off pretending it's a joke
I picked up at a service station. But it's true.

In a world of tributes, imitations, fakes,
false sightings, cover versions and remixes,
his are the lessons I should have learned

by loving him sooner, better, by listening
to the things he has to say about love,
about who to love, and who not to love.